A Thesis On The Dual Constitution Of Man: Or Neuro-Psychology

Samuel Spahr Laws

In the interest of creating a more extensive selection of rare historical book reprints, we have chosen to reproduce this title even though it may possibly have occasional imperfections such as missing and blurred pages, missing text, poor pictures, markings, dark backgrounds and other reproduction issues beyond our control. Because this work is culturally important, we have made it available as a part of our commitment to protecting, preserving and promoting the world's literature. Thank you for your understanding.

A THESIS

ON THE

DUAL CONSTITUTION OF MAN

OR

NEURO-PSYCHOLOGY,

BY

S. S. LAWS, A. M., M. D.,*

NEW YORK.

---

* "*An Inaugural Thesis* on the Dual Constitution of Man or Neuro-Psychology. Presented to the *Faculty of the Bellevue Hospital Medical College* for the Degree of Doctor of Medicine, by Samuel Spahr Laws of New York City. January 31st, 1874."

A THESIS

ON

NEURO-PSYCHOLOGY.

I.

The caption of this Thesis points to the common ground where Physiology and Psychology have been accustomed to meet, only to ignore each other's presence, or to cross swords in fierce conflict, rather than to shake hands in manly recognition of each other, as friends and co-workers, to a certain extent, in the same important field of investigation. The Physical and Metaphysical Sciences, of which Physiology and Psychology are special branches, must ultimately meet on friendly terms somewhere. Neither can hope to drive the other to the wall, for each rests on a solid and enduring foundation. The evidence of the reality and the coëxistence of both matter and mind, cannot be invalidated, respecting either, without overturning the foundations on which all knowledge rests. It is, therefore, quixotic for either to run a tilt at the other, with the view of overturning it and establishing its own pretended title to exclusive existence.

But if matter and mind exist at all, they are brought face to face in the constitution of man, and, without question, that part of man's body which is in proximate relation to *mind* is the *nervous system*. It can only be intimated here that the term *Neuro-psychology* may yet be vindicated as entitled to recognition in the vocabulary of science. There is more than one beautiful binary star in the firmament.

On discussing the phenomena of man's nervous system, the thoughts consciously or unconsciously, must necessarily move within the orbit of some one of three or four general theories of nature. 1. The first is that of the *Nihilist*, who acknowledges the substantial reality of neither matter nor mind, and in whose vision of the universe, body and soul alike vanish, as the illusions of a dream, indeed as not having the reality of a dream, nor even of the dream of a dream. 2. The second is the system of the *Idealist*, who accepts mind, but explains away, or repudiates the reality of the attributes of matter as phantasms of the senses. He holds to only *one* substance, and may be termed a *Monist* or *Scientific Unitarian.* 3. The third is the system of the *Materialist*, who pursues a precisely similar course respecting mind, by attempting to explain all its phenomena as the phenomena of matter. He is also a *Monist* or Scientific Unitarian, but his one substance is matter. 4. The fourth system recognises both mind and matter as substantial realities, each having, as to the other, its own distinctive and incommunicable properties, and resting on a footing of evidence equal with the other. This *fourth* view commends itself to the common sense of the world, and the history of opinion shows, that it has stood, like Gibraltar, unshaken by all the storms that have dashed against it. It has been aptly termed *Natural Dualism* or Natural Realism, as it looks at nature just as she presents herself, in the double aspect of mind and matter. The thirst for unity is so insatiable, as to have become an abundant source of error; and one of the most prodigious and unreasonable of these errors, is that of violating the *Law of Parcimony*, by allowing, in its application, either mind or matter to push aside the other, and to obtrude itself into the place of both.

By this law, such and so many causes are to be admitted as are necessary to explain the facts.

If a single cause or force will not do it, then more than one must be accepted as valid. It is on this principle that physicians recognise the coëxistence of several distinct maladies in the same patient, as in the case of typho-malarial fever, bronchitis associated with asthma and emphysema, or phthisis with circumscribed pneumonia and pleuritis. The concepts or "bundles of attributes," which to the mind's eye define separate diseases, will not allow us to jumble them into an indiscriminate heap, when found coëxisting in the same patient, but require us, in theory and practice, to discriminate between the phenomena presented, however intimately associated, or affected by that association they may be, and to refer them to their separate and distinct morbid conditions. It should not, therefore, seem very strange, that the exercise of the same professional discrimination, in regard to the *mixed* phenomena of the nervous system, should likewise recognise the necessity of distinguishing amongst these phenomena and of referring them to distinct and separate, but coëxistent and active producing causes. And in the proper place, it will be noted that the doctrine of a complex or dual nature of the patient is quite as important professionally, as that of a complexity of diseases.

The object of primary interest, in all scientific investigation, is a concise view of the *facts*. Theories arise from attempts to explain the facts; for, as my Lord Verulam has pithily observed, "Facts without theory, are blind." The explanation of a phenomenon consists in the reference of it to the true law of its occurrence. The identification of *mind* with nerve *force*, is a fundamental postulate with those physiologists who attempt to explain such phenomena as those of muscular contraction, sensation, perception, consciousness, memory, will, imagination, judgment, loving and sorrowing, hoping and fearing, happiness and misery, by referring them all equally and alike to the activities of mere matter, as the immediate and sole source of their production. All the facts connected with our voluntary, social, moral, religious, rational and æsthetic nature are grouped into a single category, and first and last they are explained as the products of nervous activity, the phases and transmutations of nervous energy; just as the secretions are produced by the various glands. Mental action is cerebral *ideation*. Thought, imagination, feeling and willing are forms and phases of *cerebration*.

It is perfectly obvious, that this sweeping theory, if sustained by the facts of our nervous system, settles finally man's position in nature, and his destiny forever. If these facts can by way of explanation, be thus grouped, as the phenomena of one substance, then Monism or *scientific unitarianism*, must by the law of parcimony, be accepted as the established system of nature of which *we* form a part. As physiology is one of the sisterhood of liberal and progressive sciences, and stands on the broad, fundamental principles of universal knowledge, therefore, so far as it is founded upon this unitarian principle of interpretation, all its interest in the future involves this question. Will this theory of identification stand the test of coming ages? Does it adequately respond even to the accumulated evidence confronting it in the present? Do we find in nerve-force the true and final and only law of the occurrence of this vast multitude of diversified facts?

In what shall be said in answer to this question, it is not intended to go into the general argument, against materialism or idealism as a partial and inadequate theory of man, but to limit the attention strictly to that specific point of view, under which the caption of this thesis presents the subject.

The general discussion of the coëxistence and equal substantiality of both mind and matter, is indeed very inviting, as the intellectual associations into which one feels himself brought by the mere contemplation of it are exhilarating in the extreme. For, not a few of the most brilliant, highly cultivated and thoroughly stored intellects that have shed lustre upon the history of our race, have entered into this conflict of ages, and unsparingly lavished upon it the princely treasures of their genius and acquirements. Yet strangely enough, the precise point of view, under which the subject is here presented, has been either wholly overlooked and ignored or only considered incidentally, or entered into chiefly by those preoccupied with a unitarian view. It may almost be said, that there has really been a hearing only on one side: on this side, by the mere physiologist; on that, by the mere psychologist. But who, it may be asked, has toiled in patient preparation for his work, and attempted to look with steadied and equal gaze, as a Neuro-psychologist, upon the problem, whether man be of a *unitarian* or *dual* constitution, discussing his subject in the day-light of valid evidence and not drawing on his imagination for facts? Let us hope that such investigators will be less rare in the future.

Neurology and Psychology, are both difficult subjects, and the number and discord of the laborers in each separate field, is quite embarrassing, but it is believed that the careful study of both physiology and psychology, will help to simplify both and to ultimately bring an abundant reward, in the conciliation of the two and in the consequent scientific solution of some of the most puzzling and momentous problems of life.

II.

In proceeding to the consideration in a more specific manner, of some important leading anatomical and physiological points, a concise summary will first be submitted.

The nervous matter is found in all animals, with the exception of some of the very lowest and oldest in the scale of animal life, such as the protozoans, *g. amoeba*, *g. monas*, &c., in which it may exist although as yet undiscovered. Throughout the subdivisions of the animal kingdom by Cuvier, 1812, into vertebrates, articulates, mollusks and radiates,* " the nervous system and the parts belonging thereto, as found in the perfect animal," enters into the structural type so " essentially," that it is placed at the very foundation of this great anatomical classification. The nervous element, then, is not an incidental circumstance, but a great central fact in the construction of animals. Keeping this in view, it is pertinent to observe, that there is not a precise but a general gradation of the mass and distribution of nerve matter, which places man relatively, above all other animals—I say relatively, for the brains of sev-

---

* This subdivision rests upon a principle of classification, not likely to be subverted, it is true, but, in no event, could the importance of the distribution of nerve matter, be compromised. Vide *Atlantic Monthly*, Jan., 1874. Evolut. and Perm. of Type. Agassiz' last contribution to Science.

eral animals greatly exceed that of man, in absolute weight.*

But as the interest of the present discussion centres chiefly in the nervous system of man, a more extended summary of the structure and function of that system will now be given.

The general average of the entire mass of nerve matter in the human body—estimating what is outside of the encephalos at one-eighth of the whole—may be set down at from three to four pounds avoirdupois, which would be somewhat less than the weight of the liver.† It is divided into the *gray* matter whose anatomical element is the *cell* and into the *white* matter whose anatomical element is the *fibre*. The principal accumulations or ganglia of the gray matter, are in the cerebro-spinal system and are found in the olfactory bulbs, the cerebral convolutions, the corpora-striata, the optic thalami, the cerebellar lobes, the tubercula quadrigemina, that of the pons Varolii and of the medulla oblongata; to which must be added, the cornua and the commissure of the spinal cord, the enlargements on some of the roots of the cranial and on all the posterior roots of the spinal nerves, together with the ganglia of the sympathetic system.

The distribution of the white nerve matter, is in tracts, commissures and laminations, immediately and variously associated with the gray matter or accumulations enumerated.

From these central bundles or masses of gray nerve matter, nine cranial‡ (Willis) and thirty-one vertebral, in all *forty pairs of nerves* of white matter go off, with great symmetry,

---

* Gray's *Anatomy*, p. 580. Flint's *Nervous System*, p. 340.
Brain of elephant, 8 to 10 lbs. and in specimen of large whale, above 5 lbs. The largest human brain about 4 lbs. The superiority of man's nervous organism, whatever may be the exact purpose it subserves in the economy, is not, therefore, one of mass, but probably, of texture, of specific structure, and of diverse distributions and relations.

† The rapid and large development of these two organs, the brain and the liver, in fœtal life, is a most striking fact. It may be only a superficial explanation, to point out the provision by which they are immediately supplied with best blood.

‡ Viewing the human skull as composed of 3 expanded vertebræ, (occipetal, parietal and frontal,) whose bodies in the adult are fused into the *os tri-basilare*, we would by analogy expect only 3 pairs of cranial nerves instead of 9 or 12.

and together with the sympathetic nerves, ramify to the remotest extremities of the body, supplying the skin, the muscles the bones and all the vessels and organs of the entire body, excepting chiefly the enamel of the teeth and the tendons, cartilages, hairs and nails—the parts not supplied being destitute of contractility and of sensibility. But under all circumstances, the white matter, whether in commissural masses, or in its minutest distributions, is made up of fibres which never coalesce with each other, anastomose, branch or inter-communicate, as do the blood-vessels, the lymphatics, the air-passages of the lungs, or the ducts of the liver and of the kidneys. Each nerve fibre preserves its individuality and continuity throughout its entire course.

The gray matter, in like manner, is constant in its adherence to its anatomical element, the *cell*, with its nucleus; and these cells of the gray matter, according to the usual statements, give origin to the white fibres. The deep origins of the several nerves, however, are deemed obscure. No *functional* subdivision of the gray matter is settled, although some important and interesting points of distinction, have been marked respecting the decussation of fibres and the diverse action of various excitations and lesions. But great importance attaches to the functional classification of the fibres into those that are *sensory*, and those that are *motor*.

The anatomical constituent of the ganglionic or gray matter, as seen above, is the cell, and it is now to be noted, that the specific property or function of the nerve-cell, is, according to current notions, to generate, (produce, originate,) nerve-force. This is the work of the cell. According to the current doctrine, the peculiar force or stimulus evolved or liberated by the nerve-cell, in some unknown manner, is, when liberated, then conducted by the white fibres, and this conduction of the nerve-force, is the sole function of the white fibre wherever found. The sensory fibres conduct only from the periphery inward to the central ganglia or cerebro-spinal masses of grey matter, which elaborate the impressions into ideas and volitions. These are called the *afferent* fibres. The motor fibres conduct only from the centre outward, and hence are called *efferent* fibres. But whether afferent and sensory, or efferent and motor, the capability of conducting nerve-force is the sole physiological property or function of the fibre.

For the past half century, or since Magendie's experiments, 1822, physiologists have recognised the *anterior* roots of the spinal nerves, as *motor*, and the *posterior* roots, as *sensory*. The fibres of the motor (non-gangliated) roots are distributed to muscles; and the fibres of the posterior (gangliated) roots are distributed especially to the skin. The same general physiological distribution of motor and sensory functions obtains likewise amongst the cranial nerves but on a more complicated scale. In this view, the cranial nerves may be divided into—

I. The cranial nerves of *sensation*, and these again into—

A. The cranial nerves of *special sensation*.
1. *Smell*, the 1st pair.
2. *Sight*, the 2d pair.
3. *Hearing*, the 2d root (portio mollis) of the 7th pair.
4. *Taste*.
    a. The chorda tympani from the 1st root (portio-dura) of the 7th pair, (in probable relation to the portio-intermedia of Wrisberg) and, joined with the lingual branch of the 5th pair, distributed to the anterior half or two-thirds of the tongue.
    b. The glossal branch of the glosso-pharyngeal or 1st root of the 8th pair and distributed to the posterior third of the tongue.

B. The cranial nerves of *general sensation*.
1. The large root of the 5th pair.
2. The first two roots of the 8th pair:
    a. The glosso-pharyngeal, (the 1st root.)
    b. The pneumogastric (the 2d root,) in the distribution of its root-fibres, its fibres to the mucous membrane of the larynx and epiglottis being extremely sensitive and, as Professor Flint, Jr., expresses it, "acting as a prompt sentinel to guard the entrance of the air-passages against foreign bodies."
3. The 9th pair by derivation.

II. The cranial nerves of *motion* are the 3d, the 4th, the 6th and 9th pairs, the small root of the 5th pair; and from the 7th pair, the portio-dura or facial, (except the chorda tympani,) and from the 8th pair the spinal-accessory whose spinal-rootlets give motion to the sterno-cleido mastoid and trapezius muscles, whilst its medulla oblongata rootlets make it the nerve of phonation.

It can be seen plainly enough from this sketch that the cranial, like the spinal nerves, cluster around and vibrate between the opposite poles of sensation and motion.

This general view of the nervous system of man will be rendered sufficiently complete for our present purpose, by a few words respecting the *sympathetic system*. It is identical in anatomical structure with the cerebro-spinal system and forms with it one continuous and completed whole. "The sympathetic is made up, just as is the brain and spinal cord, of cells and fibres. * * It has been unwarrantably assumed that the cells of the sympathetic system were uniformly smaller than those of the central nervous system; but it is easy to convince one's self of the error of this assertion, as cells of the largest size may readily be isolated from sympathetic ganglia. The two systems may properly be regarded as functionally conjoined organizations."*

The sympathetic contains, therefore, both motor and sensitive fibres. "The peculiarity of the sympathetic seems to consist merely in the mode in which it assembles its radical fibres, and again distributes them in the peripheral direction,"† and in the more widely dispersed condition of its gray matter, which is collected into smaller but more numerous masses, united by means of peripheral fibres.

This summary of the structure and functions of the nervous system, is perhaps sufficient to indicate the *general basis*, upon which repose the inferences, indicated above, of such tremendous import touching the constitution *of man*.

---

* Dr. Sigmund Mayer. Stricker's *Manual of Histology*, pp. 767, 768.
† Baly's Müller's *Elements of Physiology*, Second Edition, p. 715.

III.

CRITICISM AND COUNTER THEORY.

1st. The first point to which I ask attention, is that there is in the view of physiologists above stated, an exaggerated function assigned to the nerve-cell. It is assumed, throughout, as a settled fact of nature, that the nerve-cell, originally, is the source and fountain-head of all the characteristic phenomena immediately associated with the nervous system. It is the work of the nerve-cell, to liberate or evolve, by the action of its inherent and distinctive properties, and as its own peculiar product, not only volitions, which stimulate muscular action and contractions, but ideas, as well, and thinking and feeling and imagination; and in short, all the phenomena that are commonly spoken of as those of mind. Scientifically and physiologically considered, mental phenomena, properly speaking are, therefore, simply nervous phenomena and are truly explained by referring them to the single force of nerve matter.

The favorite illustration, is that of the Galvanic battery and its conductors, which device is supposed to illustrate this subject with singular aptness. The action and relation of nerve matter, nerve-cells and nerve-fibres, are thereby supposed to be pictured, as it were, before the eye. The general fact is very simple: the cells of a battery generate a force, and the wires conduct it. The wires do not produce, but only transmit the electricity, which originates from the peculiar reactions in the cells of the battery. This illustration will aid us in getting at the truth in this case. In the *first* place, it has been shown by demonstration, that the electricity conducted by the wires, actually originates from the re-action of the cells of the battery; but, it has never been shown, that the stimulus or force conducted by the nerve-fibres, originates in the nerve-cells. It has not been shown, that any of the nerve influence originates from the nerve-cell and yet it is assumed and repetitiously and dogmatically asserted that it all originates from that source. It is not *known* that any of the nerve force originates from the nerve-cell, and therefore this assumption that it all thus originates cannot be set down, and reasoned from, as a fixed fact and the most *confident* inferences be drawn from it. I do not deny, that any or any kind, of nervous influence, is attributable to the cell, as it will be seen further on, but, I protest against putting an hypothesis in the place of a *fact*. But, *again*, the actions of a battery are unique and uniform, resolving themselves into reactions, attractions and repulsions, in one settled succession or round. Whoever heard of a battery, with all its cells, in the best possible working order, its conductors and communicating appliances in perfect condition—I say, whoever heard of a battery, under the most favorable circumstances, sending a message of intelligence without an operator? The kind of force that originates from the cells and is conducted by the metallic fibres, as the result of the arrangement and combination of physical elements, can do much, but it cannot, of itself, and independent of a separate and ab-extra influence, do *that sort of thing*. The agency of a separate and superior force must be brought into appropriate and intimate relations to the subordinate force of electricity, and be capable of acting through its instruments and instrumentality before the phenomena of intelligence, of mind, will associate and blend with what would otherwise be the dull round of unrelieved physical action. It is *known*, that this strikingly analogous state of facts presented, is owing to the action of *two* agencies or forces—that its only explanation, is in the recognition of a dual source of influence.

May it not be just as reasonable, then, to explain the mixed and heterogenious phenomena of man's nervous system by a reference of them, to *two* forces as to *one*—yes, more reasonable to conclude for dualism, than for unitarianism, as the true theory of man's nature. Reasoning from the *known*, to the unknown, is the natural order and not the reverse. Even conceding, then, that the nerve-cell originates all the nerve-force proper, as the battery-cell originates all the electric force proper, still, the illustration, if of any value, suggests the conclusion, that the effects are wholly referable to that force *only* as controlled and determined by a superior force in all manifestations of mind or intelligence.*

2d. Again, the monistic or unitarian theory, as stated above, presupposes that the fibres originate from the nerve-cells; that the ganglia, are made up of these cells, as their constituent element; and that the fibres lead forth from the cells direct, or as a continuation of their poles, as the conductors lead off, from the cells or poles of a battery; or as the Croton water-pipes lead off from the Croton reservoirs and convey the water to various prearranged points of distribution. And as these pipes distribute only reservoir-water, so, the nerve-fibres convey only cell-force. But it disturbs the repose of mind that this view might reasonably be expected to give, to learn that the *primary question*, as to the relation of the nerve-fibre to the nerve-cell, is not settled; and not only so, but that the view presented, seems to be *overturned*, or, at least vitally modified, by the most recent observations. The fundamental structure of the nervous system, would appear to be the axis cylinder, which is a bundle or faciculus of primitive fibrillæ; and *the cell itself is fibrillar*,† being in fact, only *an enlargement of the axis cylinder*, caused by a finely granular substance being interspersed, or embedded, *between* the primitive filaments; and often containing a yellowish or yellowish-brown pigment. (I have here followed the views of Max Schultze, as found in chapter 3d of Stricker's Manual.) "In the present state of our knowledge, however well we may be acquainted with the peripheric termination of a great number of nerve-fibres, it *cannot be said that the mode of central origin of any single fibril, has hitherto been proved.*"‡ "No perfectly satisfactory conclusion, can be said to have been as yet attained on this point; and it is even conceivable, according to my observations, (M. Schultze) that there is

---

* It is not forgotten, that analogy is not direct proof ; but it serves to clear away rubbish, to open the mind to the exact issue and to raise a presumption, as all truth is consistent with itself. Thinking is probably more needed, at present, than new experiments and observations.

† The so-called poles are also fibrillar.

‡ This passage is quoted with approval in Gray's Anat., last edition, p. 66, foot note.

no actual termination of the fibrils in the brain or spinal cord; in other words, that all fibrils originate at the periphery, and thus *only traverse the ganglion cells.*

"The cells of the cerebrum, as I have already observed, (in other parts), possess an exquisite fibrillar structure and rather appear as a point of *junction and intersection* for nerve-fibrils that are already developed, *than as a point of origin* for those which have not hitherto been in existence."*

According to these views, and they are the last words of the highest authority on the subject, whilst the nerve-fibres may sustain an important relation to cell-substance, so called, it is made quite certain, that, in large part, they do not have cell origin; and also that it is still an open question, whether *any* of the nerve-fibres originate from nerve-cells. And if the case stands thus, then the cell must be *subordinate* to the fibre and *not* the fibre to the cell. Under this aspect of the case and head of our discussion, it may be stated, then, that the *assumption*, that all the stimulus or nerve-force conducted by the fibres, originates in the cells of the gray matter, is *not proved.* No one can pretend that it is proved. It is a mere hypothesis, to explain a supposed state of facts that probably does not exist.

3d. This modified view of the anatomical relation of the fibre to the interfibrillar cell substance, as just set forth, may warrant the suggestion, which I here venture to submit, that NUTRITION, is the proper and peculiar function allotted to the cells. The demand for nutrition by the nervous system, is *probably* greater than that of any other part of the body.

As bearing upon this idea of *nutrition* as functioned by the cell, these facts, amongst others, should be considered: viz.— 1. The character of the cell substance. 2. The relation of the gray matter to the blood circulation. 3. The amount of work done, which depends on nerve energy and causes nerve waste. 1. The interfibrillar, granular substance is probably a residue of the embryonic protoplasm, which possibly remains in greater abundance in the immediate vicinity of the nucleus, and there retains a power, allied to that which it possessed when

---

* Stricker's Manual, p. 141 : p. 139. The italics are mine.

in the embryonic state.* 2. The blood supply, to this gray matter, is estimated at five times what it is to the white nerve matter.† The ganglia or nodes, or cross roads of the fibres, are thus the depôts of supply and the places where, preëminently, nourishment and stimulus might be, perhaps are imbibed from the blood. 3. As to the work done, all muscular activity depends on nervous activity, and hence muscular waste and nerve waste would be expected to proceed with equal step. Take for instance, as an illustration, a single muscular organ, the heart.

It is a powerful hollow muscle: according to an estimate given in Flint's Physiology,‡ as "based on more reasonable data than any other," the heart, in every complete revolution or beat, exerts a force of about 75 lbs. At an average of 70 beats a minute, for an adult, this gives us over 5,000 lbs. or 2 1-2 tons a minute, and 150 tons an hour of initial force.

Respiration, is, also, a strictly muscular action. An adult makes about 16 respirations in a minute; and it has also been estimated, that each respiration marks an expenditure of force, equal to the raising of 500 lbs. one inch; and this gives us the exertion of an amount of force in one hour, that will, in that time, raise 24 tons one inch. If to this, we should add the ceaseless action of the rest of the involuntary muscles, and, also, that of the voluntary muscular contractions, verily, the result would show, that, could this force all take shape in external mechanical effect, such a worker as is the body of each man, could, in an open field, with plenty of accessible materials and *fair weather*, soon build the Pyramids. But, in all sobriety, the muscular energy exerted by the body, as a strictly physical organism, must be immense; and this astonishing expenditure of force, involves a corresponding waste or destruction and renewal of muscular and nerve tissue. The *source* of nutrition is the blood. The nerve fibre drinks in its nourishment from it, along its paths of dis-

---

* Stricker's Manual, p. 141.

† From data given in Koelliker's *Microscopical Anatomy*, (Huxley's.)

‡ *Physiology of Man, Blood*, &c., by Austin Flint, Jr., M.D., p. 198.

tribution, but especially, perhaps, as elaborated for it, by means of the interfibrillar and nucleated cell substance of the ganglia, and so, the real source of the stimulation of involuntary muscular contractility may be the blood itself, through the nervous system as an intermediary. And hence, the cell, instead of acting the exaggerated and *hyper-physiological* part assigned to it, of *ideation*, and elaborating thought and all mental activity, may find its hands full of the more natural physiological work of ministering to the nutrition of the busy fibres, as they ceaselessly functionate muscular contractility and subserve psychological as well as physiological demands.

The battery wastes, as it works, in producing electricity and it has no power of self-renewal, or it might, like the body, act unceasingly. The blood supplies the nerve-tissue its material of renewal, and hence its ceaseless action in the stimulation of the muscular activity of the organic or vegetative system. But, now, see where we stand, for the blood itself is dependent on voluntary action for the procurement and supply of its food.* We are thus brought round again by this voluntary procurement of food, as a necessary condition of existence, into the presence of mind, in voluntary activity, as a hyper-physiological force, or element, which in some form and gradation, is seen at work in all animals. "Besides the material substance of which the body is constructed, there is also an immaterial principle, which, though it eludes detection, is none the less real and to which we are constantly obliged to recur in considering the phenomena of life."†—The psychic element in man has a substratum of endowments of conscious sensation and will, in common with animals, but his specific and distinctive endowments of personality and moral agency, of rational consciousness and abtract reasoning remove him from them not merely in degree, but in kind, by an impassable barrier, by a chasm unbridged

---

* "For the life of the flesh is in the blood."—*Lev.* 17: 11-14. Gen. 9: 4. It is a remarkable circumstance that these old writings of Moses present an appreciation of the vital function of the blood quite up to modern investigation.

† *Principles of Zoölogy* by Agassiz & Gould, §128, §129.

by structural alliance. Evolution is, of course, compatible with difference only in degree.

4th. As pointing to the dual constitution of man, I wish also to call attention to the *intermediary* character of the nervous system in two other important aspects:

1st. In relation to *voluntary motion.*
2d. In relation to *sensation.*

I use the word intermediary in this sense, viz.: that, on the physiological side, in some important respects, the nervous organism is not final, but only a link in the chain of natural forces; and on the side of mind, that, in the movement from without inward, the nervous organism is only an intermediary between the external world and sensation; and in the movement from within, outward, the nervous system stands between the willing mind and voluntary muscular contraction.*

Let it be remarked that, in a word, the nervous system does not functionate for its own sake, but that like other vital viscera, it has a ministry committed to it. The forces of nature are veiled by phenomena, and if we would have a direct intellectual vision of them, we must with caution and reverence lift that veil in a spirit of "indifferency"†—not indifferency as to what the truth itself may be, but with a willingness to accept it, come whence it may, and whatever may be its bearings on preconceived opinions or interests. The watch is not understood rationally by him who only knows enough of it, to wind it, and to read the indications of time from its face. The movement consisting of a graduated train of wheels, cogs, pinions, fugee, stop, springs and escapement, mean little to the mere mechanic. All that is food for thought lies concealed from the superficial gaze; but there is in it all the beauty of a picture, to him who intelligently interprets the workings of the instrument; each part, in its place and relations, may be as suggestive as the snow-flake or the dew-drop. There is hid

---

* The mind, by its actual presence and by dynamic or catalytic or other influence may condition the involuntary activities—but of that I do not now speak.

† In the sense of John Locke, M. D., (1632–1704,) in the introduction of his great essay on the "*Human Understanding.*"

away behind the sensible phenomena in each case, a power that determined the movements, or constructed the crystal, or gave the drop of water its form.

> That very law which moulds a tear,
> And bids it trickle from its source,
> That law preserves the earth a sphere,
> And guides the planets in their course.—*Rogers.*

Whatever may be the class of the facts which we may propose to interpret, if they do not group themselves consistently under the action of a *single* force, we are bound to explain them by a reference of them to different forces, only bearing in mind that by the law of parcimony, we are restrained from assuming forces, other than what may be necessary to explain the existence of the facts.

1. But to proceed with the intermediary character of the nervous system in relation to voluntary motion. Muscular contractility, as we have seen, is an inherent property alike of striated and unstriated muscles. The involuntary muscles constitute an *automatic* system, only indirectly and incidentally under the control of the will. To this automatic system is entrusted the vital functions, so that they are sustained in sleep, as when awake. As already pointed out, the *bulk* of the work done in the economy, is done by it, and voluntary movements, as compared therewith, are only occasional and incidental and transitory, but, excepting the action of the heart, more sudden and violent. *Weariness* comes from voluntary movements only and when excessive and too much prolonged. The automatic system never tires, as it calls into play neither volition nor thought, nor directly any act of mind or intelligence. In the healthy body, there is no *knowledge* of these movements as they progress, for they are quite as much beyond the grasp of consciousness as is the law of gravitation, although we are immersed in its action continually.

The automatic phenomena are simply muscular contractions dependent on nerve-influence, and the voluntary phenomena are also muscular contractions dependent on nerve-influence. The two groups of facts are quite alike as physical phenomena but the circumstances and manner of their occurrence put us on very different lines of inquiry. Habits may cause the action of the voluntary muscles called into requisition to become allied to the automatic system, as in walking, but the main fact remains, that the voluntary activities come within the domain of direct knowledge, choice and purpose, and are not simply expressive of, but are also prompted or restrained with more or less directness and certainty, by feelings, likes or dislikes, tastes, fancies, interests, passions, prejudices, pleasure and pain, judgment and conscience—a host of circumstances, which create an atmosphere for the voluntary phenomena, so called, in which the automatic system does not and cannot breathe at all. The two spheres of activity, are, in this respect, as unlike as the earth and the moon—the one, with its atmosphere and oceans, being instinct with the conditions of animated voluntary existence, the other from this point of view, being only a dreary waste. The voluntary sphere is that of active personality; the automatic sphere is that of physical activity.* To recur again to the illustration of a battery. A system of electrical appliances, may do an allotted round of work automatically and regularly, without the active interference of an operator; and in so doing, it *remotely* evidences the wisdom and skill of the one who pre-established this self-acting combination. We are not here concerned with that remote implication, but with the fact, that a feature of the very same system of arrangements and con-

---

*Such phenomena as *blushing* from passion or the emotions of modesty, or *pallor* from fear or rage, or the *flow of saliva* from the thought or sight of food untasted, show an intimate inceptive relation between the mind and the sympathetic system to which these physiological phenomena are to be referred. But physiologically these are automate phenomena, as we are not conscious of the relaxation nor of the contraction of the arteries (*vasa vasorum*) under the control of the sympathetic nerves, which congests or empties the capillaries of the face or arouses the gland into action in these cases. It is curious to remark that there is also a broad domain of the unconscious activity of the mind, the same as of the body. It was Leibnitz who first called attention to this *law of latency* as to the mind; I am not aware that its *two* phases—physiological and psychological—have been articulately correlated. The conscious modifications of man's mind, as compared with its unconscious modifications, I have in teaching represented by a small circle inside of a large one, the small (conscious) circle having the diameter say of the axle and the large (unconscious) one, of the wheel of a carriage. The same symbol serves to represent the small amount of conscious as compared with the larger amount of unconscious activity of man's body.

nections may be such, that a present individual personality, properly endowed, and in proper relations to the system, may use it without confusion, in giving present and immediate expression to the phenomena of intelligence. All the phenomena, both the automatic and the volitional, are in this case electrical phenomena, but the circumstances and manner of their occurrence, are such as to constrain the recognition of the action of two entirely distinct forces. It would be quite as rational, to confound electric force with mind-force in this case, as nerve-force with mind-force, in man. In both cases, the *intermediary physical force* is subordinate to the action of a higher power. The muscular act of grasping with the hand is the same, whether it be to lay hold of and to cling to your own pocket-book, or to that of another. The muscular act of bending the finger is the same, whether it be to pull the trigger in the sport of the gallery, or the chase, or to defend life against an assassin, or to take life as an assassin.

May it not be asked with incisive pertinency, whether he who *sees not* back of, and above, such identical physical acts as these, the active presence of a controlling personality, of a force, entirely different from and superior to nervous and muscular force, must not be pre-occupied and infatuated by some preverse hallucination?

2. But I must hasten to consider the relation of the nervous system to *sensation.* The reality of sensation being assumed, the question arises as to its *locus.* Are the phenomena of sensation the product of nerve-action, or does the property or *power of sensation* reside in some substance different from nerve-matter? Contractility, resides in muscle, as an inherent property of its tissue. The nerve-influence does not generate it, nor impart it, but only wakes it into action, as something already existing. This contractility exists distinctly from, and independently of the nerve-influence, and may be excited by other agents, yet physiologically it is in such intimate and peculiar relation to the nerve-matter, as in some unknown way, to be excited into activity by it. Why, then, may not the power of sensation be the property of a substance quite as distinct as muscle from the nerve-matter?

It is just as easy to recognize the one alternative as the other. On the efferent, or outward movement, the power of contractility is excited *in the muscle*, by nerve-influence; on the afferent or inward movement, the power of sensation *in the mind* is excited into action by nerve-influence.

The reason of the case, then, warrants the supposition that the sensation is no more produced, nor generated, by the nerve force, than is the muscular contractility: the one, is *located in the muscle;* the other, is located *in the mind.* This, however, lands us again in *natural dualism* as the theory of man's constitution. And the reasoning that will throw down the tower of mind that stands at one end of this line of communication, will as certainly overturn the tower of muscle that stands at the other. On the one hand, the nerve-change is the physiological condition of sensation whose seat is not in nerve nor nerve-force, but in mind and mind-force; just as on the other, the nerve-change is the condition of muscular excitation whose seat is not in the nerve but in the muscle. The nerve is thus a physiological intermediary or conditionate of the muscular and also of the mental act. The connection is as intelligible in one case as in the other and the evidence of both is equally valid. The reality of the sensation in consciousness as conditioned by nerve-change is less doubtful, if there be a difference, than the reality of the muscular contraction as conditioned by nerve-action. Both are known only and alike by consciousness under empirical conditions.

But I must close this part of the discussion abruptly, as it is growing beyond the bounds of all expectation, notwithstanding the disadvantage to what has been said, that may be occasioned by the omission of a number of specific and pertinent considerations of lively interest, that have not even been intimated.

The attempt to reduce the complex phenomena associated with the workings of our nervous system to scientific unitarianism, appears to me very much vitiated by the fallacy of incomplete observation and of hasty generalization.

Whether man is a compound being, consisting of body and mind (or soul) is simply a question of *fact*, which must be settled, if at all, by the authority of evidence. That evidence is doubtless in existence and would seem to be the most accessible evidence in the world, as each one contains it completely within himself. But it is found to be extremely shy and difficult of approach.

I am satisfied, on purely scientific grounds, that not only the testimony of the senses (objective), but also that strictly on the (subjective) side of consciousness must be admitted, before the case is made complete; otherwise the case is like that of a man believing in what he sees through a microscope or a telescope, but, refusing to believe in what he sees with the naked eye. But it will be observed, that the movement of the foregoing discussion, is entirely within the sphere of neurology, that of consciousness or psychology not having been entered at all; yet, it is there, in the domain of psychology that the argument is supposed to have its main strength.

5th. But suppose the theory of the coëxistence of matter and mind, back of the complicate phenomena of man's nature as advocated in what precedes, to be conceded—and if conceded (as not contradicting the necessary import of established facts, but and only as having, in view of the available evidence, a title to serious consideration as claiming to be in accordance with fact,) then, before accepting it in full, there arise several questions, as to the *nature* and *extent* of the necessary *relation* of these coëxistent united substances, two or three of which may be considered briefly.

1. The attempts to formulate the *extent* of this relation, have been very varied, from (*a*) that of Descartes, who seated the mind in the pineal gland, to (*b*) that which holds to the *omnipresence of the mind throughout the nervous organism*—an opinion, which, in its phases, has a wonderful history, and with which, from the exigencies of the discussion in the future, physiologists may have occasion to be better acquainted, than they appear to be at present.

Some of the ablest investigators have pronounced it (*b*) "more philosophical, and, consequently, more probable than any other opinion." It was not this view of the mind's omnipresence *to the nervous system*, which was to Aristotle an undigested heap, but, of the mind's essential and indivisible oneness and indiscriminate and equal relation to the whole body that originated the peripatetic aphorism, *The soul is all in the whole* (body) *and all in every part.**

But it is interesting to note, that this view of the soul's integrity was enunciated by Aristotle, who was the discoverer of the nerves in the animal organism, and the most distinguished anatomist and naturalist of antiquity; and who acquired no less glory in philosophy, than in the sciences accessory to medicine.†

---

* "The doctrine, that the faculties and capacities of the soul, are the mere modes, in which the simple indivisible principle of thought, acts and exists, is the catholic doctrine of psychology. It is a proof of its universality, that few modern psychologists have ever thought it necessary to make an explicit profession of their faith in what they silently assumed.

No accusation can, therefore, be more ungrounded, than that which has been directed against philosophers, that they have generally harbored the opinion, that faculties are like organs in the body, distinct constituents of mind.

The Aristotelic principle, that in relation to the body, "The soul is all in the whole, and all in every part,"[1] that it is the same indivisible mind, that operates in sense, in imagination, in memory, in reasoning, &c., differently indeed, but differently only because operating in different relations—this opinion, is the one dominant among psychologists, and the one which, though not always formally proclaimed, must, if not positively disclaimed, be, in justice, presumptively attributed to every philosopher of mind."

† Dunglison's *History of Med.*, p. 129. "The principal discovery made by Aristotle, in Anatomy, was that of the nerves. But although he was well acquainted with the parts of the human frame designated under that name, he appears to have observed them only in animals.—He erroneously asserts, that there is no continuity between the brain and organs of sense, and he therefore derives all the senses from the heart."

---

[1] *Arist. Περὶ Ψυχῆς*, i. v. 31.

*   *   *   ἐν ἑκατέρῳ τῶν μορίων ἅπαντ' ἐνυπάρχει τὰ μόρια τῆς ψυχῆς, κ. τ. λ.

"In the Greek Philosophers, the term, ψυχή, (soul) comprehends, besides the sensitive and rational principle in man, the principle of organic life, both in the animal and vegetable kingdoms." The two, however, are not to be confounded. In this *Thesis*, it is after "the sensitive and rational principle in man," and *not* "the principle of organic life," that search is made.

Vide Sir Wm. Hamilton's *Lects. on Metaphysics*, pp. 271-273.

If, as is the fact, sensations be *in the mind* and not in the body, nor in any part of it, the nervous system only furnishing the physical conditions incident to their occurrence, then sensation may properly be defined, as *the mind's cognizance of any change in the nervous organism.* The change itself is not the sensation, but the mind's cognizance of it.*

There appear to be three degrees of intensity in these nerve-changes. 1st. Those that stand on a level with consciousness and come within its grasp, and so are matters of knowledge. 2d. Those below that level, as in all the processes of waste and nutrition, and the ordinary operations of the organic or automatic system. 3d. Those of hyperæsthesia. The first arouse intelligence and will, the second, leave only a diffused impression of a sense of health and well-being, when normal. But excessive excitation may occasion the intensest agitation and suffering. It is in the singleness of consciousness, that all these phenomena attain a unity and significance of higher moment, than could attach to them as the routine occurrences of an animal organism.

2. The *conditions* of the union of mind and body and of their reciprocal action are doubtless found, on the physical side, in the anatomical structure and physiological functions of the

---

* "We class *sensations* along with *emotions*, and *volitions*, and *thoughts*, under the common head of states of *consciousness*. But what consciousness is, we know not; and how it is that anything so remarkable as a state of consciousness comes about as the result of irritating nervous tissue, is just as unaccountable as the appearance of Djin when Aladdin rubbed his lamp in the story, or as any ultimate fact of nature." Huxley's Physiol. § 238.—"A state of consciousness," then, is accepted as "an ultimate fact of nature." This concession is very important, as we are not called on to explain consciousness, for we do not explain ultimate facts, but we do explain derivative and dependent facts by a reference of them to ultimate facts. We do not explain ultimate facts but we do explain by means of them. Consciousness being an ultimate fact of nature, we are no more at liberty to ignore it or to refer its appropriate phenomena to some other subject, as nerve action, than to identify the facts of pure mathematics with the facts of chemistry. Consciousness is the eye of the mind or soul, and truth is its medium of vision, like natural light to the eye of the body. Consciousness is our primary and fundamental organ of immediate as distinguished from inferential knowledge. Let us not forget nor ignore, therefore, this vital point, viz: *That consciousness is an ultimate fact of nature.*

nervous system. It is at this point, that the psychologist approaches the anatomist and physiologist, and craves his kindly help.

If it be ascertained and settled that the corpora-striata are associated with voluntary motion; the cerebellum and posterior columns of the cord with the co-ordination of motion; the optic thalami with sensation; the tubercula quadrigemina with vision, and so on—all right; for facts as *facts* are sacred, but, no theory, however current or pretentious, has the slightest validity, except as an interpretation thereof. These functions, whatever they may be ascertained to be, are the conditions sought for, upon which mental modifications or operations have, as now known, some sort of dependence. The powers of mind are not to be identified with the functions of the nervous organism, nor to be supposed inherent in the substance of which it is composed. But this organism, is the instrument, whereby or through which, as an intermediary, the mind receives impressions from without and manifests itself from within. The varied pipes, octaves and stops of the organ capacitate it to convert atmospheric vibrations, into music. But it is the musician that gives the intelligent unity of life to these vibrations.

How ghastly the contortions of the cadaver, let the excitants be applied ever so skillfully—something is lacking, the horse has lost its rider. The harp of a thousand strings lies there, and not a string is unstrung or broken, yet no music can be swept from those cords. In life, each string, each pipe, each stop and key performs its part. "If," says Dalton, "these instruments be imperfect in structure, or be damaged in any manner by violence or disease, the manifestations of intelligence are affected in a corresponding degree."* Affected it is true, but certainly not always strictly "in a corresponding degree," whether the mind be limited to the brain or be omnipresent throughout the nervous organism. The idea may here occur that, on the doctrine of this Thesis, the loss of parts of the body would imply a corresponding loss of mind or mental capacity. But it is inept. The immaterial part not

---

* Dalton's Physiology, p. 438.

being mechanically divisible, the loss of a limb is only the loss of a string from the piano or of a stop or pipe from an organ and not a loss of musical power on the part of the performer. Of course the genius of the musician cannot reveal itself beyond the capacity of his instrument, and if the instrument be mutilated, although *his* powers remain intact, yet the manifestation of them is, so far as that instrument is concerned, lessened if not destroyed. The mind can reveal itself in sensible phenomena only through its bodily organs and in the manner and to the extent only of the capabilities of the bodily organism. If legs be lost, then leg-revelation ceases, but it is only the physical ability to walk that is gone. Animals survive mutilation so long as enough of the body is left to maintain the vital functions. Consciousness remains so long as the nervous conditions of its continued relation remain. The decapitation of a frog or of an alligator* is not at

---

* "An alligator, 6½ feet long, was shot through the eye by my sister, in Lee County, Ga., March, 1865. I arrived home some two or three hours afterwards and proceeded with the assistance of a negro man to skin the animal, taking the precaution to sever the head from the body by several blows of an ax. Some minutes after this, (the head being several feet removed from the body,) I made an incision several inches long in the back of the animal near the lumbar region. No sooner had I done this than the animal gave a flounce with his tail, whereupon I withdrew to a respectful distance, to observe his movements. He then slowly and deliberately raised himself on his fore-feet, turned the decapitated extremity around to the right (the wounded side,) and shaped himself so that had the head been on he could easily have covered the wounded part. I concluded to wait until these signs of life had ceased and never repeated the experiment. (Signed,) JOHN A. WYETH."

My friend and preceptor, John A. Wyeth, M. D., (226 5th Avenue, New York, Assistant Demonstrator of Anatomy in Bellevue Hospital Medical College,) has kindly given me this statement of an interesting and important fact hitherto unpublished. It is only necessary to remark that even if the "flounce" of the tail and shudder be referred to shock or reflex action, the subsequent deliberate movement, especially in view of the somewhat exhausted condition of the animal, has probably a deeper significance. A marked sensation of a nervous change and a subsequently manifested appreciation, in accordance with experience, of an ab-extra cause to be warded off, are I conceive indicative of that pronounced phase of consciousness known as *perception*. So also the frog's appreciating and adjusting its ab-extra poise and relations, in the well known cases. It should be distinctly noted that, in the vocabulary of psychology, *perception* is sensation *plus* causation under the form of a *non-ego*; whereas in the vocabulary of the physiologist, it sometimes

once destructive of the physiological condition of the continuance of its consciousness; the decapitation of a man or of the higher animals is. This serves to intimate what I conceive to be the proper interpretation of the events and experiments to which in this connection, it is now only practicable to allude.

3. The *mode* in which the mind may act or be acted upon, through the nervous system as an organ, is just as intelligible as the mode in which the thought of the organist can take shape and be conveyed to our minds, by the manipulations of the stops and keys of his instrument. The how, may baffle comprehension, but the facts remain in their integrity.

How food effects nourishment, is an incomprehensible mystery, but the fact remains and we act on it daily. A comprehension of their mode of existence and correlation, is not, therefore, necessary to our most undoubted recognition of the reality of both body and mind in the constitution of man and as interfunctionating each other, in sickness and in health. We are competent to know that different parts of the nervous organism hold relations to the mind, different both in degree and kind; but the unity of consciousness and the oneness and immutability of our personality, which is the foundation of our identity, *preclude*, not from *relations* to the mind, but from actual or possible *identification* with the mind, all the distinctive and constitutive attributes of matter, such as extension, or diffusion, inpenetrability, division, form, weight and entire *destitution* of consciousness. It may be announced as a canon in psychology that personality has individual *ubiquity*, and that its acts must ever be somewhere, as well as somewhen, but that it only contingently respects the specific limitations that arise from the three dimensions of space, viz.: length, breadth and thickness, which hold matter in their inexorable grasp. It implies an egre-

---

has a totally different and novel meaning, viz: The ganglionic *nexus* between afferent and efferent currents in reflex action. For example, a muscular contraction, it may be in a dead body, responding to an impression upon a sensative external or internal surface is said to be perceived by the nerve centre. As the so-called perception, in such a case, has nothing to do with consciousness, it has no psychological import. Perception (proper) implies a conscious distinction between self and not self—a cognition of the ego and non ego as coexistent and correlated. It is the core of psychology.

gious misconception of the true nature of mind, about which men undertake to reason, when they, avowedly or impliedly, parcel it out amongst various parts of the nerve matter, or attempt to divide, or to distribute, or to limit it by localizing processes. The attributes of mind and of matter are incompatible and mutually exclusive of each other and *cannot co-exist in the same substance.* i.e. in the same ultimate principle or condition of unity ;* but, when each of these separate groups of attributes has found recognition as the properties of distinct and separate, substances, then their respective relations may be reasoned about intelligently. But if things so different and opposite are confounded at the very outset, stumbling thus on the threshold, only confusion, inconsequence and mistakes can be the result. To attempt therefore, to localise the mind in the brain, or in any other part or parts of the nervous organism, is beset with vicious consequences, as it is violative of the testimonies of consciousness and of experiment. These testimonies will ultimately no doubt be seen to coincide

---

* The assertion of this position, is not, as Professor Ferrier is pleased to call it, "an unshotted broadside, the brunt of which Materialism can very well stand;" but it is an impregnable fortress of truth, whose adamantine and glittering ramparts, can neither be battered nor broken, by the hostile missiles of *scientific unitarians*, whether they fight under the banner of *Idealism* or *Materialism*. If, as is conceded, the *attributes* of both mind and matter *seem* to exist, the law of Parcimony requires, not that we shall allow either to swallow up the other, but that we shall clothe each substance or object with its own qualities, as the only explanation that does no violence to the integrity of the facts of nature. The facts are patent and common property, and all acknowledge that both matter and mind seem to exist, but the difference is in the interpretation. All scientific unitarians insist, in their explanation of the facts, that this seeming is illusory and deceptive, either as to the one or the other of these substances; whereas natural dualists, adhering to the dictates of common sense, in their explanation, hold, that *this seeming* is not illusory but real and that we *actually* have in nature, just as we *seem* to have, not the mere appearances of matter and mind—not the mere semblances and shadows, but the *substantial realities*. If the seeming be wholly illusory, then neither matter nor mind exists; if it be not all illusory, then both matter and mind exist. There is no middle ground between *nihilism* and scientific *dualism*.

> Tell me not in mournful numbers,
> That life is but an empty dream,
> For the soul is dead that slumbers
> And things are not what they seem.
>   Longfellow's *Psalm of Life*.

and harmonise with the simplicity, ease and distinctness, which are ever characteristic of the truth when found. The most natural supposition would appear to be that the mind is present wherever it knows itself to be present; and this self-knowledge being a matter of consciousness, this is tantamount to saying that *the mind must be present and act, wherever it is conscious of acting.*

6th. Now, every person can test this matter for himself in various ways. *Press your toe against the floor.* You are perfectly conscious of resistance, you know it then and there, at the time and place of contact.

There is not the slightest perception, nor suggestion of currents afferent or efferent, nor of any transfer of the sensation or idea of resistance; nor is there any intimation of any lapse of time. The more often the experiment is repeated and varied, the better, as it always gives the same result.

But it is conceived to be a difficulty that the division of a nerve, or the pressure of a tumor, cuts off all sensation and voluntary motion from the distal parts. Sever the posterior roots of the lumbar and sacral nerves as did Magendie, and you may cut off the big toe or any other part of the leg on the side of the division without sensation from the operation. The division of the anterior roots destroys voluntary motion in the parts supplied and thus isolated. But this only shows that the normal *continuity* of the nerves is the physiological condition of the mind's presence and cognisance and volitional influence in those parts, and I venture the opinion that it shows and has been made to show no more. Moreover, the phenomena of reflex action cannot properly be identified with, nor made the criteria of, conscious sensation and volition.

All our knowledge, whether of self or not-self, is acquired. Innate knowledge and innate ideas have vanished like many of the fictions of physics and of physiology. Copernicus dispelled the illusion of the sun's revolution around the earth; and not till Galen did it, was it shown that blood and not air, as the name would imply, circulates in our arteries. The attributes of matter do not pertain to consciousness, and what knowledge we have of these material attributes is not innate but acquired. The magnitude, form and parts of the body, are by degrees brought within the range of our knowledge and all the facts respecting transferred sensation, as in amputated limbs and rhino-plasty, have only an *empirical* and contingent support, and the new condition of the body ordinarily soon falls within its proper associations in relation to the rest of the system. The continuity and normal physical condition of the nervous system are circumstances which cannot be violated with impunity; and established empirical associations will necessarily mislead under altered conditions until empirically corrected.

As to the theory of currents, it is by no means demonstrated. Electricity, it is conceded, is not nerve-force, and it is a fallacy to *substitute* its responses for those of nature.* I

---

* Flint's *Nervous System*, pp. 99—104. See *Popular Science Monthly*, Jan., 1873, p. 360, for a popular account of the experiments of others. This vicious substitution has hatched a brood of errors, of fallacies, of absurdities, such as that respecting the speed with which *sensation* travels along the nerves, and which fiction is in active public service, as a means of enlightening the masses! e. g.

Prof. Richard A. Proctor, in his recent course of lectures on Astronomy, credited to Prof. Mendenhall of the U. S., the honor of affording him the means of the following illustration. "Feeling is conveyed along the nerves ten times slower than sound travels. If therefore, an infant were born having an arm of the somewhat inconvenient length of 91 millions of miles, so as to reach the sun ; and if, while in the cradle in boyhood he were to stretch out his arm and touch the sun, that infant might grow to the three-score years and ten allotted to man, or even four-score, but he would never be conscious of the fact that the tip of his finger was burned. He must live 135 years before any effect would be experienced." In the same connection, and speaking within his own chosen field of labor, the distinguished lecturer urged the fact that "because there is no appreciable increase in the length of the year, it is shown that the force of gravity acts instantaneously. Gravity, the sun's might, acts, so far as we can judge, instantaneously. It is one of the forces of which we are able to give no account whatever, for all our laws of matter are opposed to the conception of force acting otherwise than by contact."

If this be so, behold the superiority of gravity to thought ! *Credat Judæus, non ego*. Electricity is very subtle, and I note very often that it misleads. Experimentations with it, like "words, are the counters of wise men, and the money of fools." Yet, on the popular theory of nerve currents, afferent and efferent, to and from the sensory, such inferences are not only legimate but inevitable however strange they may appear to be. But no theory, however plausible in speculation, can hold its ground against the facts of consciousness and the opposing light and testimony of nature herself. To ignore the direct testimony of consci-

have experimented, to my own satisfaction, with the following result. Arrange electric magnets all in the same circuit, so that a single closure may bring points or surfaces of impact in contact with various parts of the body. Fasten the magnets with their armature levers on the limbs and parts of the body, so as to make sure that the contacts with the skin shall occur; likewise average the points and degrees of contact with due reference to the variations of the sensibility of the different parts.* If the *closures are simultaneous*, then the *impressions on different parts of the healthy body are known simultaneously.*†

The consciousness or knowledge of these impressions does not arise at intervals corresponding to the distances of the parts affected from the encephalos, *but simultaneously*. If this attests anything, it is the *omnipresence of consciousness throughout the nervous organism*, cognising the changes therein at the *time* and *place* of their occurrence.—The advantages claimed by me for this experimentation are, 1st. Nature is as little disturbed as

---

ousness as primary when acting within its proper sphere, and to appeal to the testimony of instruments whose action is dependent on consciousness itself for its accuracy, is to reënact the role of the old lady who ransacked the house for her spectacles, through which she was all the time looking whilst making the search. That which is measured by the recording instruments operated by the subjects of experiments, is probably muscular contraction which, being only a mode of motion, is of course measurable, in time units; and then contingently, there may be an appreciable interval between the sensation and the volition to make the record, not to speak of the time consumed by the action of the most delicate instruments. In appreciating reflex phenomena, *the law of continuity* which I have laid down must not be ignored.

* Müller's Physiology, p. 752.

† This direct appeal to consciousness (the internal subjective standard,) must be accepted as valid, as its testimony is only checked and verified approximately by using recording instruments. If its *direct* testimony is not valid neither can its *mediate* testimony through instruments be reliable. This direct testimony is not an inference, deductive or inductive, but an immediate act and ultimate datum of consciousness. The two propositions, *I know, and I know that I know*, are, in this point of view, indentical. Every act of consciousness is self-luminous. This appeal to the testimony of consciousness direct, seems, therefore, to reduce the personal equation of error to its minimum terms. We are here dealing not only with the facts of body but of mind, and hence we must not beg the question on either side by the *method* of investigation adopted; but give all the facts and conditions in question a fair hearing.

possible; 2d. The electric action is the nearest possible approach to absolute simultaneity of impression ; 3d. There is no limit to the number or variation of the points that may be brought into comparison ; and 4th. The element of muscular contraction, a *source of palpable error*, is thrown out; and 5th, finally, even the time of the action of the instruments does not intervene to disturb the result, that is to say, there is no error in the *substitution* of the electric action, through its *appareil*, for the action of the mind itself. If the result reached be not an *illusion*, it annihilates the afferent current, and, by doing that, it overwhelms with doubt the efferent one, as physiological phenomena.

The fact, that the mind is present in the big toe and is there immediately conscious of the impressions made upon it, does not imply that the soul's energies are as fully exerted there, as where fuller and higher provisions, as in the cerebro-spinal centres, are made for furnishing it the physiological conditions of more diversified and exalted operations. That the mind *thinks in the great toe*, does not imply that it does not think also and more completely in the head; and vice versa; and the intricate arrangements of its parts, would by parity of reasoning, point to the brain as the sacred shrine where are veiled not exclusively, but pre-eminently the hidings of its powers.

IV.

I will only add, in conclusion, that the dual theory of man's constitution, has important bearings on the interpretation and treatment of morbid phenomena, and that it seems to be available as a principle of classification for what are called *Nervous Diseases*.

1st. *Neuroses.* Affections having their seat in some nerve lesion or functional disturbance, but mind not appreciably affected.

2d. *Psychoses.* Affections which have their seat in mental conditions, but body not appreciably affected. It is no more certain that some disturbances occur in the brain, cord and nerves without involving mental disturbances, than that most distressing mental conditions and aberrations occur, when bodily health is not impaired. Such cases, however, may require the Pastor rather than the Doctor, as the prospect of relief must be mainly through the mind and not the body.

3d. *Neuropsychoses.* Those affections that have their initiative in nerve-lesion, deranged function or inflammation, but invade the mind.

4th. *Psychoneuroses* begin in psychic conditions but induce nerve-lesion or functional derangement and inflammation. Facts do not appear to sustain the unitarian notion, that the mind is a mere function of the nervous organism, so that insanity and all other nervous diseases are only the expression of a morbid bodily condition. The forces that are etiological act and react in these cases, and they act from within, outward, as well as from without, inward. The bodily condition may be the symptom or the sequel, or the co-ordinate of the psychic. Mere mental depression or distress from domestic affliction, or business misfortune, sudden impressions of joy or sorrow, &c., may invade the bodily conditions on which health depends—yes, even life itself.

" Case 13,"* " A woman, aged 47, on admission, &c., gave the following account:

"Three years ago, *after a violent emotion,*† she had a feeling of numbness and formication in the upper limbs, more in the left, and afterwards in the lower limbs; gradual weakness came in all the left side, &c." Quite an evolution of progressive affections is given, evidently demanding time. " The pain went on increasing and diarrhea caused death." The author remarks respecting this case, that it is " very important, and has more value than most of the cases " related by him, on account of the microscopical examination of the altered parts of the spinal cord. " The brain and cerebellum, carefully examined, were

---

* Brown-Sequard's *Lects. on the Central Nervous System*, p. 66.

† The italics are mine.

found healthy." (Dr. Charles Robin assisted in the autopsy.)

This case began, or *took its initiative* from a purely *psychic condition*,—" a violent emotion," and the neurotic symptoms were consequent thereon, and *over 3 years* intervened before death. This was an abundance of time, for the occurrence of of all the lesions found in the examination. There is *no presumption* that any lesion *preceded* the "emotion." This, therefore, appears to be plainly a *psychoneurotic* case. The same distinguished authority, in his lectures on the diagnosis and treatment of nervous affections, places "the moral means of treatment" first in order, and observes in that connection: " I need not repeat, that I am now speaking only of those *neuroses, in which the power of the mind upon the body is so great*, that under the influence of an emotion, or another moral cause, a sudden or almost sudden *cure is not very rare.*"

The *psychic element* of our constitution, then, is not a mere function, but a functioner—a *substantial factor*, whose real and active presence cannot be ignored, in the diagnosis and treatment of disease, with any more propriety than could that of the nervous system itself.

I end this Thesis, therefore, as I began it, by invoking friendly co-operation between Physiology and Psychology, in the establishment of a Neuro-psychology, not as an abstract speculation, but as a practical philosophy, in the interest of medicine and of man.

"Dust thou art, to dust returnest,
 Was not spoken of the soul."

New York, Jan. 30th, 1874.

[N. B. As the variations from the original manuscript are immaterial, only being such as to bring out the sense in a few passages more clearly or to guard against misapprehension, they do not require articulate notice.]

Printed by Libri Plureos GmbH in Hamburg,
Germany